Living Inspired Now

Living Inspired Now

A Gift of Love and Inspiration

Shirley Colihan Premont

iUniverse LLC
Bloomington

Living Inspired Now
A Gift of Love and Inspiration

iUniverse books may be ordered through booksellers or by contacting:

iUniverse LLC
1663 Liberty Drive
Bloomington, IN 47403
www.iuniverse.com
1-800-Authors (1-800-288-4677)

Because of the dynamic nature of the Internet, any web addresses or links contained in
this book may have changed since publication and may no longer be valid. The views
expressed in this work are solely those of the author and do not necessarily reflect the views
of the publisher, and the publisher hereby disclaims any responsibility for them.

Any people depicted in stock imagery provided by Thinkstock are models,
and such images are being used for illustrative purposes only.
Certain stock imagery © Thinkstock.

ISBN: 978-1-4917-0862-0 (sc)
ISBN: 978-1-4917-0863-7 (e)

Printed in the United States of America.

iUniverse rev. date: 10/24/2013

Acknowledgements

I would like to thank my Mother Kay Colihan for her positive influence over my life, even today!

I would like to thank Jennifer S, whom I started writing daily inspirational sayings for-which created the idea for this book!

I would like to thank my husband Randy, for putting up with me the last two weeks of this writing.

I would like to thank my sister Karen Longtin for her anointed prayers over the distribution of this book!

When creating a list of good friends in my life, I came up with sixty individuals. Gracious thanks to each of you!

During the last two months of writing this book, I was so blessed to have the wonderful contributions from Anna Louise Linaur and Pete Lopez. They love the Lord with all their hearts and souls, and I thank them both! Many people are praying and believing that this book will touch millions of lives worldwide. And I thank the Good Lord, My Father Above, for His divine knowledge and power to make this happen!

Shirley Colihan Premont

Introduction

Hope, Joy, Love & Inspiration

This is a book about peace of mind which is really our truest form of expression and freedom. From peace of mind, we then have: hope, joy, love and inspiration!

We are all seeking the same thing, each and every human being, no matter what religion, race, creed, or background. It is the same. We want to have both peace of mind and freedom that will deliver us from our emotional baggage, guilt, worry or just feeling terrible much of the time!

I searched for this peace of mind for the better part of my life. I thought that I would get fulfillment when I graduated from college with a Bachelor of Science degree. Did not happen.

I thought I would have peace of mind when I got my first full-time job. Did not happen. I thought I would have peace of mind, finally, when I was the Vice President of Marketing of an organization. Did not happen.

I thought I would have peace of mind when I got married in a castle in Scotland. Did not happen.

I thought I would have peace of mind when I published my first article over twenty years ago. Did not happen.

I received my truest peace of mind, just in the past few months, very apropos for the production and publication of this book. That happened only when I fully surrendered my life to the Advocate, the Anointed One, the Almighty and the Author and Perfecter of our faith. That is our Creator!

I hope and pray the same happens to you, as you read the sayings and focus on the prayers in this book. Also note the wonderful miracles contained herein and the Intro to the Blessings of Abraham!

Now that I finally have peace of mind and joy that is unspeakable, yes, joy that is unspeakable from a heavenly source, not an earthly source, I want to encourage and inspire others!

One of my major goals, during the second half of my life, is to help others to live inspired and promising lives ~ through the faith and love that originate from Our Lord above!

And my prayer is that every man, woman and child who reads this book or listens to it, or views it via e-version will enter into this peace and freedom, living with faith and love, which in turn, will allow you to inspire others.

Chapter One
A Vision from Our Lord!

Vision: A Glimpse of Heaven

In the year of 2010, three days before Thanksgiving, I was given a vision that I am sure was meant to share with the entire world. And it is:

I was standing on the edge of Heaven. I looked down and there was a very opulent gold floor below me. The floor shone with a light that I had not seen before. The light was neither dull nor bright. It was soft and glowing and it had subtle warmth that radiated from it. It felt a bit like standing in the sunshine on a fair-weathered day, as it was neither hot nor cold but very heartwarming!

I looked to my left and saw several long strands of Mother of Pearl jewels. They were also glowing and when I looked at them a second time, they were different. They had sparkles of pink, blue, yellow and white; and the colors and hues were very soft and relaxing. I remember that I felt such a sense of comfort by looking at these pearls that formed several rows of gates.

I looked up and was allowed to walk through the gates into Heaven. It was a very short walk into Heaven and I then looked up and saw a magnificent mansion. The mansion was more like a Gothic Castle, though it had rows and rows of jewels placed in a very organized manner! The jewels were rubies, emeralds, pearls, and so on. The jewels glowed with light and opulence, though they were not overly showy. They were also soft with a feeling of contentment, and gave off such joy and light at the same time!

I kept staring at the mansion and it had no top to it. It went on and on forever into the atmosphere and I kept looking for about thirty seconds to see if I could see the top of the mansion. It had no end to it. It went into eternity.

As I looked up for the remaining seconds, I saw an extremely bright light that emanated in the sky and beyond. I was straining to see and then I saw another bright glimpse of light and a very subtle silhouette which I know was Our Lord!

I saw the new image of the light and said, "Lord, I cannot see because the light is now too bright." And the voice said back to me: "That is because you are looking with your earthly eyes and not your heavenly eyes."

There are a variety of ways that we can interpret visions given to us by the Lord. I believe this particular vision was given to me, as a very special gift, to give many people a glimpse of heaven so that people can be encouraged and know there is such an eternal place!

Prayers for Light

Creator Father, let each of us praying this prayer be a light for you and not have any darkness. Amen.

Father Above, I want to move into lightness and away from sin. Bless me to do that. Amen.

Dear Creator, what can I say as the darkness sometimes overwhelms me. I want to represent the salt and light of the world. Please help me to turn away from the world, and toward you and your commands. Amen.

Father, why is the world so evil? Teach me to live every single day with good thoughts, good intentions and goodwill to all. Amen.

Father above, please send light and truth to me today and every day of my life. I want to know simple truth that is in your Word and that will free me of burdens. Amen.

Dearest Father, give me a right perspective about life. Fill me with light, hope, joy and inspiration to overflowing! Amen.

Have you ever gone through a dark time of your life or a time or season of depression? What made the turnaround for you? How did the Lord help you during this time?

....

....

....

....

....

....

....

Chapter Two

Prayers for Your Future

Dear Father, make my future your plan implemented for me. Amen.

Our Creator, my future is in your hands because you have a good and wonderful plan for me. Even in the storms of life, I receive your grace and your blessings! Amen.

Father, what can I say? I have failed at my past and now I know that everything belongs to you. Make my future one that is upright, righteous and worthy. Amen.

Gracious Creator, sometimes I look ahead and I have fear and trepidation. Though you are not the creator of such, you want me to have hope and faith and trust in you. Thank you for this new perspective. Amen.

More Prayers for Your Future

Father Above, I have gone through some tough times in my life. And I have had seasons of worry. I want to follow you now and receive your perfect love and grace for me. Amen.

Precious Creator, I know that you will carry me through the challenging times of my life and my future will amplify what you have planned and set aside for me before the foundations of the earth were built. Amen.

Father of my Faith, I have sometimes been filled with anxiety for my future. Please remove this anxiety and replace it with hope and trust and love in you. Amen.

What are five major goals you want to accomplish in the
next five years that are important to the happiness and
advancement of your future?
How will the Almighty Lord be of help to you?

Prayers for Favor

Precious Redeemer, sometimes in my past, I thought that luck influenced my life. But you are not a creator of luck—bad nor good. You are a provider of favor, blessings and provision. Supply me with these, in every way! Thank you and Amen.

Abba Father, I want to be the apple of your eye and receive your favor always. Let my life shine for you. Amen.

Dearest Creator, I have been a recipient of your favor many times in my life, and did not know it. Know that I am grateful that you are so loving and you want to provide for your children always! Amen.

Prayers for Salvation

Father, I want to run into the hands of the one who saved me. Let me have that salvation now. I confess my sins to you and turn my life over to you now. Amen.

Father, you do not want one single soul to perish. I want to live an eternal life with you in your glory. Save me, Oh Lord. Amen.

Chapter Three

A Brief Introduction to Miracles in Our Lives

There are several people in this world who have been granted miracles. We might even think that every single person has received at least one miracle in their lifetime! I believe that the Good Lord wants to bless and advance every single person He has created. He has a purpose and a plan for every man, woman and child reading or listening to this book! The Father of humankind has many blessings in store for us. And, we have to ask, to believe, to trust and to exercise a magnificent amount of faith in that process!

Following are a few miracles granted to our other contributing writer. May they bless and encourage you immensely!

Manhattan Place Miracle

By Anna Louise Linaur, mostly reprinted from: *Then Came the Light.*

I was beginning to think that my life had no purpose, no real meaning. I had been in L.A. for one year and things hadn't gotten any better for me. I was still lost and miserable in a city and a place that was foreign to me. I hated it. My sister and I were living in a one bedroom rundown flat, on the first level of a building that had been built in the early 1920s, located on the edge of Hollywood near the old 20th Century Fox Studios. Studios that had once been a place showered with stardust, a place where wonderful dreams were made. I was residing so close to the movies and the people that had thrilled me and brought me such joy when I was growing up. But now the old buildings were abandoned. They stood as only a haunting reminder of yesterday and in just a few years they would be demolished for shopping centers and parking lots.

It was a chilly night, and all the windows in my apartment were closed. I was sitting in the living room crocheting, when I suddenly smelled smoke. Having been raised on a fear of fire, I jumped up and quickly moved through the apartment, going from room to room, sniffing out everything I could think of, and then I did it again. I ran to my front door, opening it, I entered the hallway. I stood for a moment wondering which way to go, upstairs or the lower hallway. Out in the hallway, the smell of smoke was even stronger. I started down the hall, stopping at every door sniffing and pondering the source of the smoke. After I had covered the entire downstairs hallway, I went up the stairs in the back and began the same procedure on that level. On that level, the smoke smell was no stronger or different than it had been downstairs. I stopped at every door, trying to scrutinize with my nose, what the source of the smoke could be. There was definitely something burning and I had to find the location. Now I felt a greater urgency to do so. When I finished covering the entire upstairs, my heart was pounding. Something was very wrong. I was strongly sensing this was very serious. I didn't really like my building manager, and I figured he had no great like for me, but there was something wrong. I needed to tell someone.

I knocked on the manager's door. There was no answer. It was after midnight, and I figured he must be sleeping soundly, so I continued to knock. Still no answer, and I began to feel more desperate. Finally I heard an angry voice say, "What do you want? Go away!" I told him that I was smelling smoke in my apartment and all through the building. Finally he came to the door. He came out into the hallway in his pajamas and looked around, which amounted to no more than the turning of his head. He said, "I don't smell anything." He was angry and he looked at me as if I were crazy. He said, "Go back to bed!" as he went to his doorway. I implored, "Something is wrong!" Indignant, he turned away from me, and just before he slammed the door, he yelled, "So call the fire department!"

I was scared. I had never called the police or the fire department in my life. I was still very young. What if I called the fire department, and they came out and nothing was wrong? Then would the cops come and take me to jail for being crazy? I didn't know what to do as I went back down to my apartment. Suddenly something came over me, a very strong presence, and I picked up the phone. In a matter of minutes, the fire department arrived as they were just down the street. I met them at the door of the building and told them I had called them. They said right away they could smell nothing. Several of them went upstairs, while the rest went to check out the ground floor. I went back into my apartment rather upset.

I stayed in my apartment. I was scared that I was going to get in trouble but I was still sure something was wrong. It seemed like a long time before I heard them running up the hallway and out the door. They brought in several large fans. Then there was a knock at my door. They told me they had found the source and everything would be all right. I closed the door and went back to my crocheting.

Now I heard sirens and the paramedics arrived. I don't know how much time elapsed, but it was over an hour after the ambulance left that there was a knock at my door. It was the fire captain and he asked me if I would please come out into the hallway. Next to him stood a man that I had seen come and go from the building a number of times. He was in his 50s. He was very disheveled. He didn't look well and he always looked to me as someone that was down on his luck.

The fire captain said to me, "When we arrived, we couldn't smell smoke anywhere." He said they put their hands on the doors and door knobs and down at the end of the hall, they found a door that felt hot. They broke down the door to the apartment and found the poor man that was now standing next to him, passed out on the bed. His entire apartment was filled with smoke.

The man just stood there as if he was unable to look at me. He just looked at the floor with his head down, as if in shame. I felt such compassion for him. He hadn't wanted to go to the hospital after they revived him, so after they had cleaned up as best they could at that point, the captain stayed with him until he was able to come to my door. He wanted to thank me, but he never said a word. The fire captain said, "You saved this man's life. If you hadn't called us when you did, he would not have made it." I didn't know what to say except that I knew I hadn't done anything but call the fire department. When I was feeling so useless, so unhappy, I was blessed to be a part of a miracle.

It must be noted that I was not communicating very much with the Heavenly Father at this time in my life. I was so miserable, I was really angry. Even so, the Lord was showing me "I will never leave you nor forsake you." After that night, I was no longer angry. Things began getting better for me in this new world of L.A. because I turned back to my Creator. I was so grateful that I had been there to somehow help someone. We can never know just how or when the Good Lord may need to use us!

405 Freeway Miracle

By Anna Louise Linaur, mostly reprinted from: *Then Came the Light*.

I was on the 405 freeway, out of L.A. en route to Santa Monica, California. My sister was in the passenger seat beside me. The sun had just slipped beneath the horizon, so it was still very light at about 7:30 in the evening. I was driving a Ford Thunderbird that wasn't yet two years old. That year Thunderbird was one of the best selling cars Ford ever made. It was a great car, sturdy, dependable, and safe. This evening there seemed to be an extended rush-hour, as the freeway was very congested. However, everyone was moving along at a steady clip, a little too fast for the vehicles' proximity to one another. I was in the center lane, with two lanes on either side of me. A strange, small, white foreign sports car seemed to appear out of nowhere. To this very day I don't know what that car was. Then as now, I've never seen one like it. So, it must have been a custom vehicle.

I felt very aware that I shouldn't take my eyes off this car for a moment. He was driving much too close to the car in front of him. Then he started dropping back, after which he would speed up again to the tail of the car in front of him. All of a sudden, he cut me off, and only by the grace of Our Lord, did I miss hitting him. Expecting a collision, I instantaneously swerved to the left. That set in motion a chain reaction. The car driving next to me, got spooked and hit its brakes, after which you could hear another three or four cars' screeching tires. I heard no collision, and the traffic continued moving, but I suddenly realized I couldn't get control of my car. I was careening from the left to the right and back again, down the freeway, out of control. All the cars dropped off behind me.

I'd been driving since I was 14 years of age, on everything from rain slick roads to ice covered highways. Nothing like this had ever happened to me. I couldn't get the car under control. It was as though something powerful had a hold of the car as I continued careening back and forth across the freeway, helplessly. After approximately a quarter of a mile, the car went to the left for the last time and then to the right and began heading straight for a 20 foot concrete retaining wall just before the exit I had intended to take. I screamed at the top of my lungs, "Please Dear Lord! Help us!", and only a few yards from the wall, the car suddenly stopped. As the Lord is my witness, the car suddenly stopped supernaturally. We were not thrown forward in our seats, or felt even the slightest alteration in the immediate surrounding atmosphere. I was stunned by this occurrence of His instantaneous intervention. Looking out my windshield, I could see five lanes of cars lined up as you might see at the start of a race. I knew that it was only seconds, but it seemed like long minutes as I tried to get a grip on myself. Finally, a huge semi-truck in the lane that I was straddling, anywhere from an eighth to a quarter-mile away, flashed his lights. It was as though I heard a voice in my head say, "Go ahead and get the car going. I'll cover you." The car started immediately and I noticed that, very slowly, the line of cars was beginning to descend upon me. Backing the car further onto the freeway, I was able to restore my position in the lane and then take my exit without further difficulties.

As soon as I finished my exit and was on the street, I pulled over as quickly as possible. I was shaking terribly, and as I turned the car off, I let out a tremendous burst of energy in the form of a scream, and then I began to cry. I couldn't stop thanking the Precious Lord, when I suddenly remembered my sister. Turning to her, it was as though she was just waking up. She turned and looked at me, puzzled. I had glanced at her several times during the ordeal. She wasn't afraid, she wasn't in panic, it was as though she wasn't even there. Her eyes were closed and her head seem to be bowed and she never moved or said a word. To this day, she has never remembered anything about the incident. I've seen her fall asleep on a good movie many times, but she wasn't sleeping. This was different. It was as though the Father of the Universe had completely removed her from consciousness of this horrific situation because I don't think she could have taken it. This was the sort of trauma that could cause an individual to have a heart attack. An hour later, my heart was still pounding as I continued to thank His Majesty for all his love and mercy.

I was not able to drive my usual way to Santa Monica, California, for nearly three months. As terrifying and yet miraculous as this freeway incident had been, I wasn't sure if I'd ever be able to take that route again. But finally one night, I submitted once again to the easier, quicker way. So I was taking my usual route to Santa Monica. When I reached a particular point, I knew I would soon be to the place where the horror had overwhelmed me that Tuesday evening. I am sure that something had overtaken my car, and for rather obvious reasons, I felt it had come from that little white sports car.

I couldn't believe my eyes when I got to that point just before my exit, where my car had stopped dead on the freeway, by the grace of the Holy One. The traffic was moving very slowly to bypass what must have been a very serious accident.

As I drove by that particular point on the freeway, I saw first what seemed to be about a six-foot in diameter, black charred area on the concrete wall. And then I saw what appeared to be a small mangled white sports car that they were just getting ready to remove from the scene. My blood seemed to run cold as an ardent chill swept over me. I tried to dismiss the thought that this was the sports car that had caused the trouble that night for me on the freeway. But as time passed that evening, the words kept repeating in my head, "There are no coincidences." As eerie and unbelievable as it seemed at the moment, I'm sure that mangled wreck was the little white sports car and I wondered just what had caused the devil to lose control and hit the wall, at the very same spot wherein the Creator had saved us.

Prayers for Anna Louise Linaur

Father Above, I pray that Anna Louise is always wrapped in your safety and wrapped in your arms. Keep her protected from the voices of the darkness and from voices that are not of you. Keep her in a place of comfort and contentment. Send many Angels to guard her home and her possessions . . . . Because you want to bless her in every way and keep her in a state of hope. Thank you now and in advance. Amen.

Dearest Lord, you are a good Provider and you are good all the time. Send goodness, abundance, and joy into her household for all times! Amen.

Dear Abba Father, I pray that she and her family are well taken care of. They are living the righteous lives; and your word says that "The righteous shall lack no good thing." May that verse ring so true for them. We thank you in advance and we say to you, we give you the Glory! Amen.

Inspirational Sayings by Anna Louise Linaur

"No matter how different we may be on the outside, a loving heart inside is always the same."

"Creator's love is the soul of the universe and that soul abounds everywhere."

Information about Anna Louise Linaur

~ Painter ~ Author ~ Singer ~ Philanthropist
~ Most recent book is: *Then Came the Light,* available on amazon. com, etc.

Ms. Linaur loves the Lord with every breath that she takes and she lives to promote Kingdom-Awareness. She is truly a woman of talent and one who uses her gifts for the betterment of the world and to promote the Lord's love and inspiration to all!

Chapter Four

Prayers for Righteous Living

Father, may your ways and your words be lamps unto my feet and lights unto my path. I want to be in your pathway always. Provide me with what I need to change and be under your guidance always. I thank you and say Amen.

Father—I want to be a moral example and follow your ways. Save me, now and give me that plan to live. Amen.

Father Creator, I gave my life to you and want to recommit it right now. Forgive me if I happen to stray away from your Fatherly guidance and keep me on the pathway of righteousness. Amen.

Father, I want to be ambitious in the ways that you want me to live and not to the ways of the world. Show me your ways. Amen.

Father, save me from thinking evil or thinking bitter things about another person, ever in my life! Amen.

Prayers for Peace

Father Above, I know that the peace of the Lord from the Father has been responsible for me to make progress and have favor. Amen.

Father Above, I have peace because I know that you are watching me every single day and that you are providing me with protection and care along my pathway of life! Amen.

Father Lord, I know that sin is a crime against you. Please let me take this very seriously so that I have peace and rest in the commands you have provided for me. Amen.

More Prayers for Peace

Father Creator, don't let me tremble with fear in the middle of the night. Please supply me with the peace of the Lord always. Amen.

Abba Father, may I have no fear because you have promised to give me joy and peace and clear understanding. Amen.

Dear Lord, when I sin I am fearful of facing the Almighty. Please show me the tenderness of life and the righteousness of life and let me live by these precepts! Amen.

Father Above, I do not want eternal death as I want to be judged according to my deeds and by the grace you have provided me.
Please give me a peace about the salvation that you have provided for me, through your Son. Or please show and provide me with that salvation, through the sources and the people available to me! Amen.

Chapter Five

Prayers for Understanding and Decision Making

Father, I want to make the right decisions to live a righteous life. Be at the helm of my decision-making. I do pray. Amen.

Father, I yearn for clarity of thinking when I have to make small and huge decisions in my life. Be the one who directs and prompts me to make the best decisions so I may stay in the very center of your will and plan. Amen.

Father, I want to be your child of light and life. I want to have much understanding for the kingdom. Amen.

Father, please fill me with your wisdom and understanding. Please keep the darkness away from me, this day and always. Amen.

Father, I have enormous decisions to make with impact and potential repercussions. Help me to focus on the ways of the Lord during those times and always. Thank you in advance. Amen.

More Prayers for Understanding

and Decision Making

Dearest Lord, I know that you want me to follow your heart and your divine inspiration. Divinely and supernaturally inspire me when I have to make life decisions. Amen.

Father, because the spirit has been sent to convict the world of sin and judgments, help me to face you with a sense of clear understanding and wisdom and forgiveness toward others! Amen.

Prayers for Change

Father, please change me and mold me like the potter forms the clay. I ask for your help and restoration in this process. Amen.

Dear Lord, don't let me change when I need to pray and ask you for guidance. Your guidance and your direction are keeping me in the places that you want me to be, temporarily. Please keep me in the precious plan you have designed for me. Amen.

Heavenly Father, I have to change because I am not living always to the precepts and commands you have set forth many years ago. I want to hear your voice in my spiritual ears as you are changing me. Thank you and Amen.

More Prayers for Change

Dear Lord, change has gripped me with fear. Please take away any and all fears I have felt due to change. Fill me with joy and trust and let me rest in your protection. Amen.

Father Above, you are loving and just and want to change my life. One touch of your hand will change my life forever more. And I ask that today, and always. Amen.

Abba Father, I want to change to live a highly moral and righteous life. Fill me with the spirit of the Lord that operates in love and joy. Amen.

Dear Lord, I do not want to live eternal life in punishment. I must change to know that I have been saved and taken into your kingdom. Please be just toward me, as I change now. Amen.

Because judgment is coming and you are a just Creator, please bring the gospel and all of the good news to us. Make a way for us, all of us reading this,—to escape harsh judgment. Change us from the inside out. Amen.

Chapter Six

Prayers for Joy

Father, some of my life has been filled with strife, with disappointment and with crises. I yearn and long for a joy-filled life, which you and only you can provide. Outpour your joy into me as I await this change. Amen.

Father Creator, why do I not have the joy you promised me? Please remove the conditions and obstacles that are in the way of me receiving the heavenly joy you have planned for me. Amen.

Abba Father, I want to have both peace and joy that exceed all understanding. Please grant these to me, as I believe you have them for me. Amen.

Father Above, the joy of the Lord is a perfect joy. It is pure, relaxing, honest, carefree and filled with heavenly peace. I want to live my life in that joy. Please keep me in that spiritual state now and forever more. Amen.

More Prayers for Joy

Father Above, before I knew you and had a relationship with you, my life had dark thoughts and heavy oppression. Now is the the time I want to be your child, and I want to live within your amazing joy. Amen.

Creator above, I want to live as you would have me to live and that will bring me peace forever more. Amen.

Dearest Creator, I think it is odd that I had no peace until I found you. When I find this to be true, you have overwhelmed me with the reality and radiance of your peace that passes all understanding!
Amen!

Father Lord, I know that you have called me to be your child and to live in your kingdom of light. That gives me the peace that I need and will live for. Amen.

What are three things that you can do that will create more joy and peaceful living in your life?
What steps and items do you need to complete to attain the joy for which you long?

Chapter Seven

Prayers for Light and Peace from Above

Dear Lord, light comes through you and you alone. I live in the kingdom of light because I have peace, joy and truth that only originate from you. Amen.

Dear Lord, place a moral compass inside of me that will keep me in your light and peace and keep me away from all powers of darkness. Amen

Heavenly Father, I have been open to your guidance and want to have the peace that you provide to all of those who live under your law. Amen.

Lord, when I come in contact with the darkness of the world, let me know that your peace guides and directs me through these worldly imperfections. Amen.

More Prayers for Light and Peace from Above

Dearest Father, I have peace because I know that you have given me all the resources and provisions I need for my entire lifetime. Amen.

Dear Lord, what shall I do when Our Lord rises up and I come in awareness of Him? I pray that I should have peace now about my facing The Almighty later. Amen.

My Creator, may I have no fear because you have promised to give me joy and peace and understanding. Amen.

Dear Lord, when I sin I am fearful of facing The Almighty. Please show me the tenderness of life and the righteousness of life and let me live by this. Amen.

Father Above, I do not want eternal death as I want to be judged according to my deeds and by the grace you have provided me. Please give me a peace about the salvation that you have provided for me, by your cross. Amen.

Chapter Eight

Prayers for Hearing the Lord's Voice

Dear Lord, I long to hear your voice that will confirm things that are happening in my life. Your word says that we have not, because we ask not. I am asking you today for an anointing over my life to hear and see you as even more real to me. Amen.

Dear Most Gracious Father—I would like to hear from you with clarity and certainty. That is my prayer. Let it be known to me, through signs and wonders from above, of how I may hear your voice and hear you speaking to me! Amen and Amen!

Father In Heaven—What a privilege it will be for me to hear your voice and to know you better. I want to spend special time with you to do that. Allow me both the focus and the time to do so. Thank you and Amen!

Abba Father, Please block out the daily distractions when I go into my prayer time with you. I want to hear your voice in a crystal clear way that is telling me how you much you love me and how you want to bless me! Amen.

Dearest Holy One, the day is ahead of me in which I will get to know you in a magnificent and amazing way. I long for that day, and pray it will be very soon. Amen.

Visitation/Encounter: The Garden of Eden and Miracles Pete and the Yahwah Revolution

In June of 2013, I was very tired from a very long day of work and was having dinner around 9:30pm. As I was having dinner alone, I sat and prayed. I noticed the chair on the other side of the table was out and facing toward the kitchen to my right, as though someone was in it. And I said, "Lord, you're here, right?" And He said, "Yes, I am." And immediately, my strength returned! And I laughed and said, "I know you are here, as I can feel your presence." And I started praising and thanking him for *everything*. And I started asking questions about past events, like was He there when my daughter fell out of the window of the second floor of our two-story apartment, years ago, when she was only one. And I said, "You caught her, huh?" He said, "Yes, I did." I asked about the time I almost drowned and numerous other things. I mentioned to Him that I should have died a long time ago, and I said, "You saved me every time and You were always there, thank you." And just like that, He gave me a revelation of the Garden of Eden . . . !

At the time, I had been studying the Garden of Eden for about six months. He said, "The Garden is in the spirit realm and we can no longer see it." And I was just in awe of this and thanked Him! And we both said at the same time—that our eyes are spiritually closed. Then He told me that He put an angel leading to the Garden to lead the way back in. And

I said, "And that's right and a flaming sword!" He said "yes" and I said: "That's great, Lord, thank you for telling me. And He said that He had put that in my heart. I said, "Yes, I know you did, thanks Lord, I've been studying the Four Rivers and the Garden for a while now and you came to tell me this!" I continued, "You're awesome, how wonderful is that, Lord, ~You know people won't believe it!"

He then said, "It's for you, Son. And I said: "Thanks Father, you're the best!"

And, it didn't seem like a very long time as I then did my dishes, brushed my teeth and went to bed. As I lay in bed, all of a sudden, I stopped speaking to the Lord. Instead I started thinking about the next few days and how I was going to get things done, etc. Then I thought, Oh My Lord, I am so sorry,— . . .How very rude of me and I'm very sorry. And He said, "It's all-right son, you're only human, and I love you, it's all-right!" And I felt better and then I said good-night.

The next day, my daughter texted me and said that she saw an angel in her room right after praying. I asked her, "Are you sure?" She said, "Yes." I asked what it looked like, and so on and so forth. And then I told her that was a coincidence, as I was with the Lord also last night! I asked what time it was, and she indicated that it was between 9:30 and 10:30pm. We concluded that it was about the same time, and we praised the Lord!

For those reading this, please make time in your lives to talk with the Lord because He is real and He will sup with you and talk with you!! You only need to start a conversation with Him! Test this and see. You have nothing to lose, and everything to gain! I bless everyone reading or listening to this book. May the Lord prosper you in all things! Amen.

Chapter Nine

Prayers for Love

Dear Lord, for The Father so loved the world that he gave his only son. Let me have the peace that I do know that I will live in eternity with you. Amen.

Father Above, we know that your love is perfect and that your justice is just as perfect as your love! Let me know your love, your justice and your grace always! Thank you, Lord. Amen.

Dear Creator, you are perfect in all of your ways. Let me love your gospel and your word, so that I can live in love always. Amen.

Information on Bitterness

Bitterness can harm you mentally, physically and spiritually! Remember to look into your heart, once again, and search for any bitterness you may have. Ask the Spirit of the Lord to remove any bitterness you might have harbored within ~ knowingly or unknowingly.

Replace bitterness with love!

Discuss how you would feel if love was flowing through your life every single day and you displayed love to others most of the time, daily?
What do you need to do to make this a reality? Be very honest here.

Chapter Ten

Prayers for Your Eternal Plan!

Heavenly Father, help me to die to myself and find the plan that you have for me. Amen.

Dear Lord, what is the answer for my life? I need more than what the world has planned for me. Amen.

Dearest Benefactor, you have the answer for me to know the bigger plan for my life and the specifics of each and every day. Teach me those elements and show me your ways, not mine. Amen.

Dear Lord, so much of the world trusts the map of human wisdom. Let me know your wisdom and your plan for me always. Amen.

Father in Heaven, I want to live with wisdom and understanding that come from you above. I want to know you more and have a relationship with you. In that way, I will get to know the ways and directions you have planned for me. Amen.

More Prayers for Your Eternal Plan

Heavenly Father, I have had a rough start to my life, but I want to have a clean and holy finish to my life. Amen.

Dear Creator, let me reach out to others who need to know your plan for their lives. Amen.

Dearest Holy One, I want to follow you and you only. Teach me, instruct me, and anoint me daily. Amen.

Dearest Father, I want to be of the elect of the Lord. I want to be chosen by you for all of eternity. Thank you and Amen!

Important Question: Do you, with all certainty, know where you will go when you die? You need to have this assurance to live the blessed life.

What else do you need—or whom can you go to to help you have the assurance of this?

Chapter Eleven

Prayers for the Lord's Direction

Lord, I want to be chosen by you always and change as you want me to change. Amen.

Our Father, I want to be holy and beloved and set apart by you. Amen.

Dear Lord, I am your handiwork and your masterpiece and you are showing me the ways to go. Amen.

Dearest Holy One, you know the thoughts of mine and everyone and you know the intentions of my heart. Help me to have pure thoughts and pure intentions. Amen.

Father Above, I don't have to worry about my own agenda because you are in control and in command of my life. Amen.

Dear Lord, I want to surrender it all to you, as then—I will have the peace and understanding that surpasses all. Amen.

More Prayers for the Lord's Direction

Dear Lord, I choose to trust you and be humble as you work your plan through me. Amen.

Dear Abba Father, please give me patience with people, as you show me your ways. Amen.

Dear Lord, I want to gain all you have for me and be alive. Don't let sin reign in my body. I want to be free. Amen.

Dear Holy One, I am under grace and not under the law and want to be free. Amen.

Dearest Lord, why do I sin against you? Teach and instruct me the right and righteous ways to live! Amen.

Chapter Twelve

Prayers to Be Anointed

Dearest Father, don't let me be tied to my temper nor my weaknesses. Do not allow me to fail in your process and the plans you have for me. Amen.

Dear Lord, I want to be set aside and sanctified for you. Please work in my life as I triumph in you and keep going in those righteous ways. Amen.

Dearest Creator above,—send your spirit to live in me. That will help me to rest in you as you do the work that needs to be done. Amen.

Dear Father, please teach me to be of the righteous and the selected person that you plan for me to be. Amen.

Dearest Holy One, I want to live on the roadmap of my life that you have compassed for me. Amen.

Dear Lord, please teach me to be joyous as others receive the blessings that you have selected for them! Give me patience to turn the right way each and every day. Amen.

Prayers for Quality of Life

Father Above, please guide me to live and turn your way always. Please teach me to be patient and giving each day as I live the way you want me to. Amen.

Dearest Lord, I want to have harmony in my life. Show me how to thank you for the love and armor you provide me each and every day. Amen.

Lord, I want to live a life of moral quality that is the way you want me to live. Amen.

Prayers for Seeking the Lord's Heart

Dear Creator, please teach me to be a person who is after your heart, always. Show me to live in compliance with your will. Amen.

Dear Lord, let me live in your own nature not in the nature of sin. Amen.

Holy Father, I want to have the opportunity to live a life that will be a good legacy and that shows goodness and righteousness always! Amen and Amen.

More Prayers for Seeking the Lord's Heart

Dear Lord, teach and show me how to do all of your will. Show me how to know and experience you more each day. Amen.

Creator, I know that man looks at the outward appearance, but that you look at the heart of humankind. Plant the true word into my heart so that I will live your way. Amen.

Prayers for Living a Surrendered Life!

Dear Lord, I choose to live a life for you. Give me the tools to do so and to surrender to your will. Amen.

Father Above, I want to delight in your ways always. You have told me if I delight myself in you,—you shall give me the desires of my heart. Amen.

Dear Lord, let me be pliable to you, let me surrender myself over to your will. Amen.

More Prayers for Living a Surrendered Life!

Father, I want to surrender all. I want to yield to you for what you want for me. I want to have you in my life—your will and your will only and always. Amen.

Dear Creator, you have told me that if I ask anything, according to your will I will have those petitions asked and they will be answered. Amen.

Father Protector, protect me and save me and forgive me from my blunders of my life. Amen.

Father, when I do sin against you, rise me up immediately to your presence and your will again. Amen.

Dearest Creator, I don't want to live with fleshly and humanly passions and desires. Teach me to live the righteous life every single day. Amen.

Precious Lord, I know that there is a battle between the flesh and the spirit. Show me and lead me to the ways of the spirit from above. Amen.

More Prayers for Living a Surrendered Life!

Dear Lord, I don't want to give in to my sinly natures or sinful desires. Please send your spirit and your grace to keep me in line with your precious word! Amen.

Father above, my mind is very complex and I want my mind to focus on you and your word always and all the days of my life. Amen.

Dear Lord, I thank you that you graciously supply me with all the resources, sources and provisions that I so need, once I surrender my life to you. Amen.

Father, I want to always surrender myself under your will. Amen.

Heavenly Father, I want to align my life with what you have planned for me and for what your will has designed for me. Amen.

Do you believe that you have surrendered your life to your Lord and Creator? Why or why not?

....

....

....

....

....

....

....

....

....

....

....

....

Chapter Thirteen

Prayers for the Goodness From Above

Dear Lord, you do love me and you want to keep me away from danger and from sin always and all the days of my life. Amen.

Father Lord, I do have a sinful nature but I want to give back to you the some of the goodness that you have given to me. Amen.

Dear Lord, I know that you want my heart and my heart alone. That is what you want from me. Let me offer my full heart to you always and all the days of my life. Amen.

Dear Creator, I want my heart to be filled with thanksgiving all the time! Amen.

Dear Lord, I know that you desire my worship. I want to call upon the name of the Lord always. Amen.

Dearest Father above, I want to live all of eternity with you and now I want to live my life for you with purpose and passion. Amen.

More Prayers for Goodness from Above

Father above, my mind is very complex and I want my mind to focus on you and your word always and all the days of my life. Amen.

Dear Lord, I want to live in your goodness and receive every good gift from above that you have ready for me to receive! Amen.

Father, I want to have every good and perfect gift from above and not necessarily those of this world. Show me how to live with this difference and to be receptive of the joy and goodness you have for me! Amen.

Heavenly Father, I want to align my life with what you have planned for me and for what your will is designed for me. I want to live a life free of worry and emotional pain, and receive your goodness and mercy every day. Amen.

Chapter Fourteen

Prayers on Peace, Judgment and Redemption

Dear Lord, let me have the peace and comfort that passes all understanding as I plan to live my life for you. Amen.

Dear Creator, please do not let me judge the mistakes of others or the mistakes of myself. Please let me know that you see my heart and you look beyond my mistakes. Amen.

Dear Lord, I want to be remembered as a person after your own heart. I do not want to judge others ever; and I don't want others to judge me. Amen.

Dear Lord, I was born into this world into sin, though I know you want me to live a righteous life that seeks you and seeks your will for my life, first and foremost. Then I will be precious onto you. Amen.

Do you believe you are living your life according to the Lord's will?

Why or why not? What do you need to do to find out more information on this? Whom can you talk to about this? Think clearly and make this an important priority in your life!

Prayers for Forgiveness

Father Above, Please forgive me for my sins of the past and wash me clean, I pray. Amen.

Dearest Lord, take away anything in my life that is not of you and your precious will. Amen.

Abba Father, I wish to be of one accord with your will for my life. The Bible says that you hold my very breath in your hands. That is an awesome thought and I pray you show me that this is true for me! Please forgive me when I make wrong choices! Amen and thank you.

Dearest Creator, You have made me to respond to your love for me, and I confess that sometimes I have not lived the best way I could. Make that right for me now, I sincerely pray. Amen.

Father in Heaven, I want to live a life that gives love and joy to others and does not harbor feelings of unforgiveness for anyone. Teach me to live that way, I do seek and pray. Amen!

Lord on High, I seek to be free of any anger that has ever been in my life, knowingly or unknowingly. Wash that away with the spirit and keep me in a state of pure thoughts of love and compassion toward all! Amen.

Dear Holy One, My life has sometimes had some anger or ill will toward others. Today is the day that I ask that you wash that fresh and anew and make me of your pure thinking and your genuine thinking! Amen and Amen.

Finally Father, I want to know that you have forgiven me, so I will indeed believe that to be true and feel the cleansing and the purity of my soul—which only you can provide to your children. Amen.

Ask for wisdom to be given to you from the Holy Spirit. Then search your heart to see if there is anyone, living or deceased, whom you have not forgiven? If so, repent of this and ask the Lord to cleanse you of this feeling forever more!

Prayers to Live According to the Lord's Will

Dearest Father, Teach me to fulfill your plan, your desires and help me to become the person you want me to be! Amen.

Creator, please do a spiritual work inside of me and complete it in me, and I give you the glory for that. Amen.

Dear Lord, I want to discover the will of Our Creator and do all that you want me to do. Amen.

Dear Abba Father, I know that you have a marvelous plan for me and I want to fulfill that plan, one day at a time! Amen.

Dear Lord, I am thankful to you that I have surrendered my will to you, and now I can rest in you alone. Amen.

Dearest Father, I want to follow the examples of those people in the Bible who have led and lived after your own heart. Amen.

Prayers for An Excellent Life

Dear Father Above, please do not let me sink so low that I live in sin. Amen.

Father Lord, we are all born with human passions and desires. I do not want to live after those things, though I want to live for you. Amen.

Dear Lord, let the spirit of the Lord lead me, prompt me, teach me, and show me the ways of the Lord. Amen.

Dear Creator, let me know when you are warning me of the fact that I am in the wrong place or doing the wrong thing. Amen.

Abba Father, when your hand of providence is over me and showing me the way to go, I see the prosperity you have planned for me! Amen.

Dear Father, what makes me happy is what makes you happy. Show me your goodness and your love, so I may show that to others. Amen.

Chapter Fifteen

Prayers for Hope and Joy

Father, I have a bright future filled with hope and goodness. Teach me to walk in your ways to find this hope and goodness. Amen.

Father, my life has been somewhat disappointing at times. And, I now know that as I live the life of living for you. I will have hope in this world and hope that is beyond measure in the next world. Thank you for this assurance. Amen.

Dear Lord, what is the best gift that you can give us? It must be hope in you and hope in the future. Amen.

Father above, I cannot live my life without hope one more day. I pray for the hope and the life that is everlasting and eternal. Amen.

Dear Lord, may I have joy, hope and remembrances of all good things above and beyond what I now know. Amen

More Prayers for Hope and Joy

Dear Lord, my hope is in you and in those things that last. I know that this life is just a vapor, before all of eternity. Teach me to be aware of your bigger plan each and every day of my life. Amen!

Dear Precious Creator, I desire to know you better and then I can know hope and joy and those things that are of higher meaning. Amen.

Dear Lord, may the overall hope and peace that pass all understanding be mine today and forever more. Amen.

Creator above, I seek to have a life of hope and joy! I seek to receive your grace to teach me how to live in a hopeful manner and in a joyful way. I seek these from you now. Amen and thank you!

Chapter Sixteen

Prayer for Cindi: Father Above, we pray for the protection, peace, provision, redemption and love for all of the children in the program. We pray that many will help the efforts to rescue, care for, raise, minister to, and love these precious children. We pray you pour out your strength and your resources among every part of this project! And we pray that all involved will receive special blessings, an abundance of resources, and spiritual restoration beyond measure!
In the name of your son, we pray. Amen.

Prayer for Vance: Dearest Lord Above, we pray that Vance will be an amazing adult and will have an amazing life of success and many victories! We pray that his education will excel beyond measure and that he will be an expert communicator! We pray that every blessing of Abraham is his ~ to live an abundant and prosperous life. In the name of our precious savior, we pray. Amen.

Prayer for My Mother, Sisters and Brother: Dearest Lord, we thank you for the incredible blessings you have given us! We pray that the lives of each family member will be blessed with; goodness from above, light and life always, and wholeness in health, spirit, soul, mind, and body. We pray for harmony and abundance in their households. And we pray that the touch of the Lord's hand and truth will forever prevail. Amen!

Prayer for My Nieces and Nephews: Precious Lord, we pray for their protection, their success and every victory in lives. Let them lead courageously, while they follow Our Lord, to fulfill their lives.

In your only-begotten son's name, we pray. Amen.

Prayer for Adam Alexander: Dearest Lord Above, we pray that Adam Alexander is blessed all the days of his life! We pray that his Mother and Grandmother are always walking in grace, happiness, wisdom, understanding, favor and provisions from above! We pray laughter, harmony and abundance into their households. Amen and Amen.

Prayer for Delene: Father God, always provide Delene with your safety and your guidance. Keep her in an element of strength and energy and vitality always. Bring harmony and joy to every area of her life! Let her know how much you love her and how delighted you are of her service to others and her gift of encouragement! Amen and Amen.

Prayer for Sheryl: Dear Lord, let Sheryl shine with more talent, more enthusiasm and more success in her life! Send many provisions, much favor and abundance into her current and future households! Let her have peace of mind and laughter and good health all the days of her life! Amen and Amen.

Prayer for Jerome: Father God, always use the wonderful talent and gifts you have given him for the Glory of the Kingdom and its Righteousness! Keep his family safe, protected and generously provided for all the days of their lives! Touch them with renewal and your guidance each and every day. Amen and Amen.

Prayer for Lisa, John and Daughters: Dearest Lord, we pray that this family will always have much guidance, discernment, creativity, energy and good health! We pray that you will renew and instruct them daily. We pray for their households to be filled with joy and abundance. And we pray that they will have freedom from anxiety in their daily living. Amen and Amen.

Chapter Seventeen

Inspirational Sayings on Daily Living and Success

We need to celebrate the success of others, our own successes, and then we will know true joy!

When we are tired or low in energy, let us stop and think of "how positively changed the future will be" because of our efforts today!

Do not let your future be plagued with worry. Know that the battles belong to the Lord and so do the major wars of life! Let us turn each of these over to the Lord.

Your future can be bright if you know To Whom your future belongs!

Each person contributes to the outcome of their future by good intent, good work and good follow-through!

Keep your future as a source of hope and goodwill.

When the future looks bleak, ask the Creator to change and He will make the turnaround, because He is the author of turnarounds!

Know that the future is filled with joy if you have given your life over to the One who made you and this world and everything in it.

Inspirational Sayings on Time

We must always guard and use our time very judiciously!

Time can never be retrieved, so use it with good wisdom and love toward all others!

Time is our friend; and procrastination is our enemy!

Time can be used most efficiently when we are calm and collected and in a state of grace!

Time cannot be stolen from you, without you allowing it to be taken!

Inspirational Sayings on Worry and Guilt

Worry and guilt have no productive or positive place in our lives.
We should ask Our Creator to remove any traces of them.

Worry and guilt pile negative input into our souls and our minds.

Worry and guilt bring the potential for ill health!

Worry and guilt are no longer part of our life system. They are the roots of bitterness and toxic waste!

Worry and guilt rob us of total happiness and joy from our Creator!

Internal strife, caused by worry or guilt, is toxin to our body and soul!

Chapter Eighteen

Inspirational Sayings on Wisdom

The more wisdom you receive, the more you are expected to help and complete others!

The storms of life, grow not only our faith,—but bring great wisdom!

The wisdom from above is a thousand times more precious than gold, silver and all the jewels of the universe!

Once the Creator grants you wisdom and favor, your life will change to be exponentially enriching, forever more!

The more Heavenly wisdom we have, the more we must exercise discretion!

The preludes to wisdom are: revelation knowledge, trust and understanding.

The more wisdom we are given, the more challenging our life will be!

The less wisdom and faith one has, the more one will experience the painful voids in life!

What areas of your life do you need to develop more wisdom?
And, how will this help you to live a more fulfilled and blessed life?

....

....

....

....

....

....

....

....

Chapter Nineteen

Inspirational Sayings on Change

You cannot change the community or the world, until you change yourself!

We can desire change, but it won't happen, until we pray and take action.

Change can bring about great growth and development, as long as we have an open mind and embrace these changes!

And if you are willing to change:

Pray this prayer today ~ Dear Father Lord, I am sorry for my sins. Wash me clean and forgive me of them. Make me whole and new again! Take over my life so that I can live for you and surrender to you! I believe that your Son has come to save me and give me eternal life. Amen and Amen.

Inspirational Sayings on Prayer

Prayer is talking and listening to the Creator of the Universe!

Prayer can be enlightening and fulfilling for us,—as we pray for others and their intentions!

Praying cleanses the soul and opens our communication with the Father above!

Praying, with a pure and sincere heart, will reap more answers than we can ever imagine!

The simplest prayer, with a simple and true heart: "Save me, Dear Lord" is life-changing!

Remember to pray for others who are in any type of pain! Remember to pray for others who cannot pray for themselves!

Once we start praying consistently, our spirit will be filled with awe and wonder!

More Inspirational Sayings on Prayer

We cannot have wickedness or unforgiveness hidden in our heart–if we expect our prayers to be answered!

Pray with a pure heart and a simple tone, and our Abba Father will certainly hear you!

Pray as though . . . you have no tomorrow!

Pray for every nation of the world—
Pray that the people of this world will ask for forgiveness, change their ways—and then the turnaround from our Creator will take place!

Send your prayers to heaven with the purity of a child and a love for humankind!

Keep remembrance of those less fortunate than yourself and pray for their intentions daily!

Pray that the leaders of the world will receive heavenly wisdom and seek counsel from the Almighty!

More Inspirational Sayings on Prayer

Keep praying until your spirit is filled with peace and contentment.

Ask angels to be dispatched and sent on your behalf. Pray for the safety and protection of every person in this world!

When you pray, know that the Creator of this world is listening with an open ear and the longing to bless you more!

Keep lifting up the underprivileged and abused children of this world, and pray for their protection and refuge!

Prayers will remind you of the multitude of blessings you have been given!

Prayers will open up the doors of heaven for miracles!

Prayer, with faith and action, will allow the windows and doors of heaven to open to your intentions and the intentions of many!

Discuss your current prayer life or the prayer life you would desire to have. Ask for wisdom and revelation knowledge right now!

_____

_____

_____

_____

_____

_____

_____

_____

Chapter Twenty

Prayers for Wisdom and Knowledge

Dear Father above, I want to have heavenly knowledge and wisdom so I can live in a way that is pleasing to you. I want to know truth and wisdom from the word of the Lord. Grant my desires. Amen.

Dearest Lord, give me knowledge, discernment and wisdom that will change my life and those of others around me so I will be blessed and be a blessing to many others. I pray for this intention. Amen.

Abba Father, the wisdom from above is more valuable than rubies, jewels and all the precious things of this world. Surround me and fill me with this wisdom. Amen.

Father, I would like you to give me the knowledge that I need to live my life with success all around me and to share my knowledge to the betterment of others. Amen and Amen.

Creator, I pray for knowledge in all areas to help my country, to help my fellow man, to help my family and to help all those in need. Amen.

Father Above, please give me the knowledge of King Solomon and give me the discernment that you know is best for my life and my situations. Amen.

Dear Holy One, I need to know the wisdom and discernment and judgment that are created by you for all of those who seek you and your face. Amen.

Chapter Twenty-One

Introduction to Genuine Faith and Blessings

We all live in a world that is sometimes blurred with confusion, obstacles and other hindering elements. Though, let us all realize that there are blessings for each of us and **these are supernatural**, not of the natural realm! Everything we have that is sustainable, long-term, that exists in this natural world is first in the spirit, or first takes place because of FAITH. Faith is not just a feeling; it is an actual belief or revelation from our Creator.

So then, seeing something in a supernatural sense comes first from seeing it in the natural sense. Our mind is certainly able to see what we need to know or believe as faith. When our minds are blind-sighted, we do not see what the Creator has in store for us. Revelation of knowledge is then what changes us and changes the world.

If we can see something, smell it, taste it, etc, using our senses, it is subject to change. Though, in the supernatural realm, when we have something that becomes a blessing, it is indeed here for all of eternity!

Let us take Abraham, in the Bible, as an excellent example.

Chapter Twenty-Two

Background: Blessings of Abraham

Depending on how they are counted in the Bible, it has been noted that there are either seven, twelve or forty blessings of Abraham. We are focusing on the main Seven Blessings of Abraham here!

We learn that these blessings **are also available to all the children of the Lord.** And, we should know that the blessings to follow are available to all of those who are ingrafted through him (Abraham) by faith! Abraham is a perfect illustration, in human form, of our Father in heaven. Our Father genuinely wants nothing more than to bless us in every way! In speaking of the Bible overall, when we as His children, have a special, personal need—Our Heavenly Father has promised to fulfill it!

We must continuously remind ourselves that Yahwah (The Lord) wants to bless His children spiritually, physically, emotionally and financially!

And back to Abraham! Yahwah (the Lord) told Abram, his name at that time, to leave his country from his father's house—to go to a land that He would show him. Genesis 12:1.

And in this scenario, the Lord's blessings were dependent upon Abram's level of faith and trust in the Lord! Abram had to decide whether or not to accept Yahwah's calling to leave the idol-worshipping country that it had become.

In our own personal lives, the Lord of all, asks us to stop worshipping idols that are either false or substitute gods, as well. Look into your own life to see if this makes sense to you and ways that you can change to serve the Lord more fully and faithfully!

Simply stated, then, these are the Seven Blessings of Abraham to explore here. In our next book, *Living Inspired Now, Two* there will be greater detail and more comprehensive knowledge on these blessings.

The Seven Blessings of Abraham
This section is written by Pete Lopez and the Yahwah Revolution of Houston, Texas. The Blessings are as follows:

1) **Make him into a great nation;**

2) **Bless him immensely;**

3) **Make his name great;**

4) **Make him a blessing to others;**

5) **Bless those who bless him;**

6) **Curse those who curse him; and,**

7) That all the peoples of the earth would be blessed through him.

There are many examples that we can learn from Abraham's life! Though the main elements we should grasp are that through him, meaning through his Hebrew bloodline; and his faith in the Lord's promise to bring forth a son—are the cornerstones of faith. So that, through our faith in Him (Yahwah), we will be continuously blessed!

The main elements are that: 1) Abraham, as a father, was just a picture of what was to come! And 2) The Spiritual Father (the Lord) used Abraham to return us to Him through His Son Immanuel—meaning the Lord is with us.

Blessing Number One. I will make you a great nation. Abram's wife Sarai was unable to have children, and she was 90 years old when Elohim (Hebrew for Lord) promised them a son. Abram was 99 years old. Speak of a true Miracle! They had Isaac the very next year when Abraham was 100 years old and Sarah was 91. They also received their new names, Genesis 17:1-15.

Blessing Number Two. Bless him immensely. Elohim (Hebrew for Lord) blessed Abram in many, many ways. Here are a few examples. He gave him children at a very old age. And also, when the Prince of Pharoah took Sarai into his household, Elohim plagued the Pharaoh's house so they couldn't have any children. And Elohim got her back for him, and then the Lord made Abram rich in sheep and cattle and donkeys, male and female servants, and camels, etc! Genesis 12: 14-20.

Blessing Number Three. Make his name great. All religions recognize Abraham all over the world. Have you heard of Abraham? Every person has, to be sure!

Another point of this passage is that—when the Creator tells Abram that his name will be great—He is saying that Abram will be fulfilled mentally, socially and spiritually. As children of the Creator of the universe, we are all entitled to this same blessing!

Blessing Number Four. Make him a blessing to others. One example of this is through Abraham's nephew Lot. In Genesis 14:11 and 12, Lot is taken captive. Abraham put his 318 well-trained servants into action, went to war and took all the men back completely unharmed!

He also interceded for Lot and his family. And the Angels of the Lord Yahwah saved them from the destruction of Sodom and Gomorrah. What an uncle, what a blessing!

Blessing Number Five. Bless those who bless him. One prime example of this is from after the war in Genesis 14:18-20. The King of Salem (also the priest) gave Abram bread and wine and blessed him. The king Priest then received a tithe or a tenth of the kingdom's possessions. One tenth may not sound like much; however, this was a tenth of four thriving kingdoms at that time! What a blessing!

In our everyday living, we can see how this works as well. The Good Lord continuously blesses us as we bless other people. The circle of blessings just grows and grows. Watch this happen in your own life!

Blessing Number Six. Curse those who curse you. One need not go far from the book of Genesis Chapters twelve through 25, to see this. Probably due to the blessing over Abraham's life, you probably won't find bad or negative things about him! However, in actuality, there are those who are unknowingly doing just that—by not excepting Abraham's family and the One that came through him—Yahwah Elohim. Every time someone came up against Abraham or his family, Elohim delivered them!

Blessing Number Seven. And in you, all the people of the earth should be blessed. For this blessing, we go to the New Testament! One need not look any further than the blessed Apostle Paul! He said:
"The Scripture foresaw that Our Lord would justify the Gentiles by faith, and announced the gospel in advance to Abraham: All nations will be blessed through you." Galatians 3:8.

Do blessings upon all nations lessen the blessing of Abraham's physical family? No, not at all! If, however, the descendents of Abraham relegate the Gentiles to a status that is separate and distinct from them, and not an integral part of their family— then Gentiles being blessed would rival and cast a shadow on the unique character of the Blessing on Abraham's family.

On the other hand, if Abraham's family embraces the Gentiles, allowing them to be part of their family, then the blessing remains unique. It rests on the entire embodied family! Paul insisted when he said: "Understand them, that those who believe are children of Abraham." Galations 3:7. And another version states: "You may take it, then that it is those who have faith who are Abraham's sons (and daughters)." Also note, "So then, those who are of faith, are blessed with believing Abraham!" Galations 3:9.

~~ End of Pete and the Yahwah Revolution's contributions ~~

Information about Pete Lopez:

- Old Testament Scholar and Teacher
- Founder of "Pete and the Yahwah Revolution" of Houston, Texas

Mr. Lopez restores classical cars as his livelihood, though he lives to create "Yahwah-Awareness" worldwide!

~~~~~~

"Our Father so loved the world that he gave his only Son, that everyone who has faith in him may not perish, but will have eternal life."

John 3:16

Author Note:

I want to end this book with an important saying that is simple and profound from Anjali Verma, which is: "Remember to take wonderful care of yourself. Then you are able to help multitudes of people along your pathway of life."

And finally, the prayer we have for each person reading or hearing this book is: you will be filled with the Spirit of the Lord, you will receive more hope, joy, love and inspiration than ever before, and you will always have the Blessings of Abraham in your life!

The End

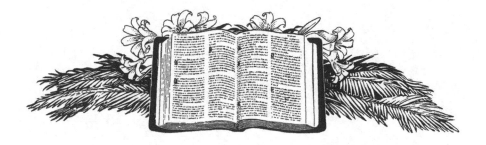

Sources include: The MacArthur Study Bible, The Revised English Bible and other translations of The Holy Bible.